"I am the Lord's treasured jewel."
Malachi 3:17

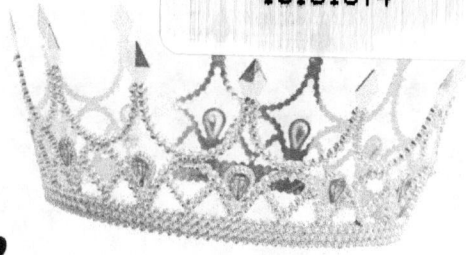

Jewels
IN HIS CROWN

God's chosen treasure set apart, called out of darkness, and claimed as His very own. You shall walk in His grace, mercy, and marvelous light.

LASHONE STRICKLAND

Jewels In His Crown
Copyright 2025 Lashone Strickland

Paperback: ISBN 979-8-991-4825-2-3
Ebook: ISBN 979-8-991-4825-3-0

Published by Tymm Publishing LLC
Columbia, South Carolina

Book cover design: TywebbinCreations.com
Editor: Darcy Werkman

CONTENTS

Love Letter

To my precious Lord Jesus Christ, who is my Lord and Savior. I will always love, cherish, and honor you. I, Lashone Strickland, say yes to your will in my life. I say yes to your commandments. All my praise and worship go to you, Lord. If I had a thousand tongues, it wouldn't be enough to thank you for all your bountiful blessings. I celebrate you every day of my life and for all eternity. When my eyes open as I awake, I say, "Thank you, Lord." My heart leaps for joy for the brand-new mercies that you give to me each morning.

I am so blessed to be called a daughter of the King of Kings. I am one of the Jewels in your beautiful royal crown of glory. I am a beloved child of the Lord, my Heavenly Father. Thank you for specially making and designing me.

You shed your blood for me on that old rugged cross. You gave your life as a ransom for many. This was the sacrifice that paid the price for our sins, allowing us to be forgiven and reconciled with God (1 Peter 3:18). That's what kind of God you are. A selfless, honorable, righteous, and loving God. There is no greater sacrifice than that! You are the Holy Trinity, the three in one—Father, Son, and Holy Spirit. The Father in Heaven, who is the creator of all things (Genesis 1:26). The Son of God, who was sent to save us from our sins (Matthew 1:21). The Holy Spirit, the Helper whom God sent as a gift for us now on earth (John 14:26). This is the ultimate gift for me and my family. My family and I receive you by faith and prayer. I pledge allegiance to you, Jesus. I look to you as the Lord of my life. I invite your Holy Spirit to live within me at all times. I love you indefinitely and for eternity, Lord Jesus!

With sincerity,

Your daughter who is a Jewel called to be in your crown.

Author Lashone Strickland

HONOR

I would like to take this time to honor our spiritual mom and prophetic prophet pastor, Linda Anderson. I give honor to you for being an outstanding teacher for the Father. Some of us have watched you for many years and have learned so much. You are a true example of being a woman of God. The prophetic anointing God has given to you is a rare gem. You only get this gift and anointing from spending quality time with the Father. It takes obedience, discipline, patience, dedication, determination, and sacrifice. When you stir all these ingredients in one pot, combined together, this makes greatness. Pastor Linda, your name is in that pot. God is giving you the Crown of Life.

In the Bible, the Crown of Life is a symbolic representation of eternal life and is awarded to those who faithfully endure trials and tribulations in their faith, essentially signifying God's recognition and reward for perseverance through hardship. It is most commonly referenced in James 1:12, where it states, "Blessed is the one who perseveres under trial because, having stood the test, that person will receive the Crown of Life that the Lord has promised to those who love him." The Crown of Life also represents the ultimate reward of eternal life in heaven.

Pastor Linda Anderson, you have been found faithful. God is pleased with your work in the Kingdom. God loves you dearly. Thank you for all you have done for me and all of God's children. You are truly amazing. Jewels for Grace (J4G) honors you, and I honor you. Most importantly, God is rewarding you. You are a spiritual mom to so many.

Being a spiritual mom for J4G is a complete blessing. We are women who love God with our whole heart. God has placed us in His crown. When we talk, we light up His crown. It's the anointing that we carry. The more we lay at His feet, the more radiant His crown glows. God trusts Pastor Linda with the Jewels in His crown. She prays for the Jewels. She joins us in our fasting and prayers. She gives financially and donates her time. She supports our fundraisers and all our charity giving. She has advertised all of our events. She does a lot behind the scenes to help Jewels for Grace be a blessing to those in need. Pastor Linda is very near and dear to our hearts. We will love her for eternity.

Sincerely,

Jewels for Grace

PURPOSE

The purpose of me writing this book is to share the blessing and gift that God has given the women of Jewels for Grace, namely the gift of grace, mercy, and unconditional love. It is the gift that keeps on giving when you are in covenant with God. His anointing and Holy Ghost fire have been given to Jewels for Grace. I want to share who each Jewel is individually, in their own uniqueness and spirit, as well as share how this women's group got started and information on what we do. I want to introduce the Junior Jewels and the discipleship God has graced us with in the hope of being an inspiration to other women. I pray that God gives them the desire and blessing to help encourage other women in their own unique way. There is always work to do and lives to help change forever. It's all for the Kingdom of God and His glory. Jewels for Grace is a light for the Lord Jesus Christ. He is our great foundation.

Being Jewels in His crown has been a special blessing and gift from the Lord. I hope this will be inspiring for other women of God, bringing women in all truth to be set free from all captivity. I pray that they can become the example of women who lift other women up by adjusting their crown and never bragging about it. This will bring glory and honor to God. "Therefore encourage and build each other up, just as in fact you are doing" (1 Thessalonians 5:11).

ACKNOWLEDGMENTS

To Jewels for Grace husbands: Garnell, Tony, Mark, Jerome, and Will. We thank you all for loving your wives and supporting them by giving them time to serve. May God spark an everlasting friendship, love, and fire in your marriages.

To Jewels for Grace families, parents, stepparents, children, and grandchildren. Smile, because your Jewel for Grace—a lady of the Lord—is shining. Parents, you brought her into the world. She is truly a generational blessing to her family. Children and grandchildren, you reap the benefits of being loved by this Jewel in His crown. She is a perfect example of a mother in Christ Jesus. Glory to God in the highest. She is a rare Jewel in His exquisite crown of light and hope.

INTRODUCTION

My natural mother, Carolyn Young, was chosen by God for my sister, Jewel Bonita Irby, and me. God doesn't make any mistakes. She was the one chosen for us. Everything is for a purpose and a reason. The Father gave our mother a beautiful gift, which was to be a loving mother, a nurturer, a protector, and a worshiper of God. God blessed her with two daughters. God has blessed her with double. A child is a gift from God no matter what the circumstances are when conceived. Being called to be a mother is an important and high calling.

Mom, not only did you accept the gift to be a mother, but you also protected us in an unusual way. We didn't get to go to some places growing up. As a child it seemed like we were different, and it didn't feel good at the time. You had rules that other parents didn't have for their children. Some would say that it was strict. I say that you were being a lady of wisdom. You understood your assignment with your daughters, which was to keep them safe no matter what the world was doing. You did what was best for us.

For example, you didn't let us spend the night with people. As an adult, it's hard to try and explain to your kids why they aren't going to sleepovers and slumber parties. All you can do is tell them it's for their protection. As a child, I didn't understand. I just wanted to go, especially with kids I went to school with. It seemed so unfair because all my friends were there. Now, as an adult, I hear horror stories of what some kids endured, and I am forever grateful for what you did for us.

To this day, we take those same values and instill them in our children. You created a generational blessing for our family, just by being a protector for your children.

Your daughters will forever love you. Bonita and I will take what you taught us into future generations. Thank you, Mom, for all you have done for us. It takes a brave woman to do what you did. I pray that God continues to give you direction. You are the mother of light and truth for our family. The kids love their Grandma Sista. We will all love you always. "Children are a heritage from the Lord, offspring a reward from him" (Psalms 127:3).

My sister and I, Jewel Bonita, are natural sisters. We share the same blood. We have the same mother and father. Starting out young, we were just like natural siblings. We fussed, fought, and got on each other's nerves. Sibling rivalry, the whole shebang—that was us. I wanted to be an only child. I wanted all the attention. To be honest, I was a spoiled brat. I didn't know what I was doing. I just needed some guidance on how to love. Bonita and I are nine years apart in age, with her being the older sister. She let me know that she prayed really hard for me, because she was really lonely. She finally got what she wanted, but they say to be careful what you pray for.

She wasn't happy with this new package she got. Her response was, "Where can I send this back to?" Her life was flipped upside down. She didn't know that, because of her age and maturity, she was going to have to help take care of me. When Mom had to go grocery shopping—and let's be honest, babies don't belong there, especially when the weather is cold—who do we guess had to stay back and do the diaper changes? The older I got, the worse this was for her. *The baby can walk and talk now. Wait, I have to share a room with my younger sister?* These were all Bonita's thoughts.

Bonita was a teenager and wanted privacy. One of Bonita's chores was going to the laundromat. Who do you think had to go with her? At first, I was too young to help, but by the time I was in the sixth grade, she started training me on washing and folding clothes. She got so good that she also trained two of my cousins, Anitra and Xavia. That way if one couldn't go, she would call the other. Anitra and I laugh so much to this day, because Bonita would pull up on us and say, "One, two, three . . ." This meant to do it fast and good. So we would hop in her car real quick, and Bonita would set us up at the laundromat. She would say, "One, two, three . . ." and we would be ready to do laundry. We often tease Bonita and say, "One, two, three . . ." and laugh about it. We tell her we can't believe we fell for that. Now she makes it seem like it was fun and not work. In reality, it was enjoyable because my cousins and I would have a fun time hanging out waiting on the clothes. There was a game room in the shopping center, so we would put the clothes in the wash and go over and hang out. Some of our friends and some new friends would go there with us. We absolutely cherish our childhood memories.

There was another thing Bonita had to be responsible for being an older sister. In order for me to go to the skating rink, my sister had to go. This came from our mom. I really loved the rink. My eyes became quite busy with all they had going on. This was a learning experience and pretty interesting to me. I became a tagalong. To my sister, it felt like I was her child, which was quite alarming to her and made things a little rocky growing up. But in the midst of the storms, God always has a bigger picture and plan. Trust in Him at all times. "Trust in the Lord with all your heart and lean not on your own understanding; in all your ways submit to him, and he will make your paths straight" (Proverbs 3:5-6).

As we got older, Bonita graduated high school, and boy, did my plans change. I saw things differently now. I was in middle school, and from then until high school, I was the best dressed. She let me wear some of her clothes, so I had a double wardrobe. I would also sneak some of her stuff out of her room before she returned from work at night. She never knew until now. As I grew older, I really started to admire her for so many things. She was responsible and smart, and she had a nice car. I always wanted to ride out wherever she was going. Her and her friends lived a fascinating life.

Bonita stayed in the house with us until she was twenty-five years old. When she got her first apartment, I was there every weekend. And when she had my nephew, I loved him so much. He was the first baby in the family since I was a baby sixteen years earlier. What Bonita was to me growing up, I most certainly was to my nephew. She didn't have to worry about anything when it came to him. I even got up in the middle of the night to help. I was in high school by this time.

The funny thing about the first ten years of my life is that I didn't see clearly about her. She was my older sister who I absolutely had nothing in common with. We were not compatible at all. But remember, God always has a plan that is better than ours. I started to see value ten years later. The funny thing is that it was now turn for Bonita to not see the value in our relationship for the next ten years. I was just her little sister who had a lot to learn. One thing about this: she did love me. Once I graduated high school, I moved right in with her and her two-year-old son. I stayed a year until I got married. I was only eighteen years old at the time.

Bonita sees me as a little sister that she loves, not just a best friend or a sister in the Spirit. These things take time and patience. We had to let it grow into what God wanted it to in time. We have seen a lot and been through a lot, and we always had each other to lean on. We became mothers, wives, and most of all women of God. With this we have finally discovered that we are twins in the spirit. In the natural realm, we are women who aren't perfect. We love naturally and wholeheartedly. In the early years of our life, we were just discovering who we were in this world. We had to grow through so much. The spirit realm looks different than the natural realm. We are just grateful to know the difference between the two.

Bonita has some of the same gifts as I do. We think a lot alike. We even sometimes end up at the same places when we haven't even discussed anything, especially restaurants. Or we'll pick out the same card for family members, like for a baby shower, birthday, wedding, etc., or we'll pick out the same gift bags at stores. And we only find out because at the party it's the same gift bags. We find that we are doing the same stuff all the time. We are on the same wavelength. This is a spiritual thing for sure.

If you have faith, you learn to understand the spirit world. You can't physically see this with your natural eyes. This may be difficult for some people. This is where the Bible comes into play. Read it and pray for God's true revelation and knowledge of the Word. If you knock, He will answer. In the spirit realm, we are greater than the physical, which is a natural realm. We are engaged in spiritual warfare. Bonita and I are prayer warriors. We are called to intercede for His people. We have discovered so much together on our spiritual journey. We come from a long line of women in the Spirit. Our grandmother had three sisters and a sister-in-law who were powerful in God. The Willam sisters left a great legacy of children who reference and honor God for eternity. I know that there are some other Jewels that come from a long line of ancestors that were great. We are honored to be a part of it. Today looks different than the times back then. The key is understanding what day and time we are in.

Live for today and not in the past. What worked then may not work today. It's always a new game plan to keep switching around.

Peter warns us to be alert and aware of adversaries. "Be alert and of sober mind. Your enemy the devil prowls around like a roaring lion looking for someone to devour" (1 Peter 5:8). Being ignorant of Satan's devices and tricks can be of great harm to the believer. There are a number of energy forms we can't see, yet they do exist. Wind, electricity, and gravity are all energies you can't see. "Put on the full armor of God, so that you can take your stand against the devil's schemes. For our struggle is not against flesh and blood, but against the rulers, against the authorities, against the powers of this dark world and against the spiritual forces of evil in the heavenly realms" (Ephesians 6:11-12). The longer we do not understand how the spirit world works, the longer we are giving the enemy legal access to our life. We have to know the rules of the playbook in order to win. I don't care how good you speak in tongues. I don't care how faithfully you go to church. You still will be bound. The goal is to have you and your family free from bondage. Sin is a high cost to pay. The enemy's job is to keep you bound. Resist the devil and he will flee.

Let me brag on my God. The God I serve set the moon to revolve around the earth, and He set the earth to go around the sun along with other planets. My God is a deliverer, healer, and provider. He has so many names. All my glory goes to El Shaddai, meaning God Almighty. Jehovah Jireh is a name for God that means "the Lord will provide." Jehovah Nissi is a name for God that means "the Lord is my banner" or "the Lord my victory." The name "Jehovah-Rapha" translates to "the Lord who heals." I have learned to call on Him. He is the author of my life, and no matter the circumstances, all things work together for my good (Romans 8:28).

God always has a plan for Bonita and me. Some people may not understand this, and they may even question it or poke fun at it. *Why do they always have to go everywhere together? You don't see one without the other.* We live seven houses away from one another. Our house ain't ever running out of sugar. Bonita's husband, Tony, jokes and says he doesn't want my advice because I think too much like his wife. You can literally put us in a different room and ask the same question, and we will give the same answer. My sister and I accepted this gift from God. We know where we came from. It is quite healthy for siblings to be this way. This is how we are twins in the Spirit. In nature twins feel this way and act this way. They are conceived at the same time and born together. Twins bring something different and special to the world. Everyone admires twin siblings.

The God I serve can change things and make you unusual or out of the ordinary, which can bring jealous spirits. Jealousy is a negative emotion or feeling you get when someone has something you want. People often fear the unknown, and they have difficulty accepting what might be an amazing gift for you. They tend to want what they can't have, especially when it feels out of reach for them. It's a selfish way to feel. You don't know what a person went through to get the blessing.

Blessings don't have a name on it. You have to put your name right there. Claim the blessing and confess it and pray the will and Word of God. Let your energy be positive and fight for you and your good. Get rid of the negative energy that works against you. I don't think God designed families to grow up in the same house for eighteen years or longer just to go into the world and not be a part of each other's life. You may eventually have a family of your own. Make a decision that the brokenness stops here. Your family will be a generational blessing. Your beginning never matters. What you decide to do with the broken pieces determines your outcome.

Our God is a master. He can put the tiny pieces back together. I am a woman who has had her heart broken into pieces. I have had the worst beginning. Despite that, there is always someone who has it worse. Focus on the now. Stay in the present to get to your future. Your children should build bonds with one another. Family support is so important. We are the branches to the family tree. God is our root and foundation. If this isn't your family's background, God can change things for you. He can repair the broken branches. Family love and support is needed in this world we live in. Unity and one accord holds so much power. It's being a team for your family. We all bring things to the pot to help each other. It's never one-sided.

God isn't calling you to be misused. Know the difference between being appreciated and taking advantage of. God wants you whole and your family whole. Your family dynamic might look different than mine. You may not have a sister, but maybe you have a mom that you can really bond with, or a brother, or maybe even your children or an aunt. God gave us all at least one person. If it looks different than my family dynamic, it's okay. I would never be jealous that you are a daddy's girl. That's your family blessing that looks different from mine.

My sister's kids are my kids and vice versa. That's family love, and it's unconditional. I understand if families haven't started from a foundation rooted in these things. My sister and I have made an agreement that it stops right here. This goes for all generational curses in the family bloodline. One bloodline family curse is shyness. A great deal of our family don't like to talk, especially in large crowds or with people they just met. God didn't give us a spirit of fear but of love and a sound mind. Anything else is not of God. We are to immediately cast those thoughts down.

Get good at recognizing family patterns. Be a curse-breaker for your family. It stops with you today. To break a curse you need to repent of anything that you or your family bloodline did to allow the curse to be at work. If something was done and gave it a legal right to be there, repent of it. Next, you will need to renounce it and divorce that covenant. Finally, you are to replace it with a new covenant of blessings with the Father. Pray and ask God for a prayer partner. You only need one other soul that is a born-again believer to agree with you and war in the spiritual realm and fight for your life. You can always get in agreement with the Holy Spirit. The Holy Spirit is a friend to you. There is so much power in that alone. Thank God for leaving us with the gift of the Holy Spirit. We do not wrestle against flesh and blood.

Let's pray for our families to have Abraham's blessings in their life now and forever (Genesis 12:1-3). God promised Abraham that He would multiply his descendants as the stars in the sky. He would be their God and give them a specific piece of land forever. God blessed Abraham with seven blessings. We know that seven is a number of completion. He promised to make Abraham a great nation. He promised to bless Abraham. He promised to make his name great. He said that Abraham will be a blessing. He promised to those who blessed Abraham that He would bless them, and whoever cursed Abraham would be cursed by Him. Everyone on earth will be blessed through Abraham. The same God will do this for our families. I decree and declare the blessings of Abraham on your life and your descendants.

Please Pray Aloud

Dear Lord, I come to you asking for forgiveness of my sins and your children's sins. I repent of everything that's not like you, including negative thinking. I repent for family bloodline curses—for anything that I or anyone in my family bloodline have done. I ask that you heal families inside out. Give your children knowledge of who they are in you. Let them know their true identity and worth. If it's a desire to fill their love tank with family that's not around, please be a great guide to them on where to start to mend their families' branches again. If this isn't your will and you need to protect them, I ask that you show them and that they have the heart and mind to receive it. If it is your will to let a miracle transform into something beautiful for their family, I pray that they have the love and support that's needed. All things are possible to him who believes. I pray that you send them a strong prayer partner, someone that you have designed for them. I ask that you remove stumbling blocks or hindering spirits. I ask that you bless them with the seven blessings of Abraham. May you bless them richly and add no sorrow. I am so grateful for all of your goodness. I praise your holy name. You are

God alone. There's no limit to what you can and will do. Thank you, Father God. You are better than good. Words cannot express my feelings toward you. There is no greater feeling or love or emotion than to have you, Lord. I love you, Lord God Almighty. I ask for family blessings for your children in the name of Jesus. Hallelujah and Amen.

INSPIRATION

Bonita and I were a part of a women's Bible study group years ago. Our spiritual mother, Pastor Linda, was leader and founder of Predestined Women. This was a group of women who traveled locally to meet and have the most empowering encounters with God. The power of God was there, and the Holy Spirit was always there. True deliverance took place. We learned so much about God. The information and knowledge grew us so much in the Spirit. We studied the Word of God. We all gave powerful testimonies on what God was doing in our lives. There were always fresh topics about exactly what was needed. It ministered to our souls. Also, each woman brought a dish, and we ate good afterwards.

In addition to this, Pastor Linda has started Women on the Wall. This is another powerful ministry led and founded by our spiritual mom. This is a group of women on a Zoom call. It's very similar to Predestined

Women, but it's in the comfort of our own homes. It works because in the days and time we live in, we can meet people where they are at. The Zoom calls are so powerful. We study the Word and have powerful prayers and testimonies. We fast and pray and spend time with God. We love God and honor Him. We freely love and forgive our neighbors. Pastor Linda also runs a powerful women's conference, which is incorporated by Women on the Wall.

These ministries have absolutely changed our lives forever. Not only us, but it has also changed the lives of so many women of God, and all because of our spiritual mom being obedient to God. Being sensitive to His voice, she is helping shape and mold the lives of His daughters. We honor Pastor Linda Anderson, and we love her dearly. Our spiritual mom has so many daughters. The anointing that they carry is so sacred. What's on the head flows down. Being a mother is the most important role that He has given. Being a mother doesn't only mean your blood. It's much bigger than that. It's something about the Father in Heaven trusting you with His children. Someone that is empty needs your anointing to be delivered, healed, and set free. Building a legacy of women that have the power of God that moves mountains will destroy every yoke of bondage. This is the very example of our spiritual mom. I'm so proud of all the gifts inside of her.

Being a spiritual daughter to Pastor Linda means we reap benefits. This is a Naomi and Ruth encounter. Pastor Linda is Naomi to many, many women of God today. She is building women of noble character. If you don't know the story of Naomi and Ruth in the Holy Bible, take some time to read it or refresh yourself of it. The book of Ruth expresses a woman following another woman serving her God. Her loyalty granted her so much favor. We never know what descendant will come through our bloodline. Because of Ruth's obedience, history has been made. When you make God your business, you are truly in the will of God. "Trust in the Lord with all your heart, and lean not on your own understanding; in all your ways submit to him, and he will make your paths straight" (Proverbs 3:5-6). This shows God that you trust Him.

Bonita and I have the same heart as our spiritual mother. Remember, what's on the head flows down. Mix yourself up with the right ingredients. What are you baking? What seeds are you planting? Pastor Linda is seeing those seeds that she watered with the Word of God. Through her perseverance and determination she has birthed many things in the natural realm, which took place in the spiritual realm first and have manifested in the right now. Glory to God! Bonita and I have talked about Predestined Women and how it stuck with us and changed us forever. I reminded her about how we received a prophetic word years ago that women would be laid out on our living room floor by the Holy Spirit and that miracles and transformation would take place, and that's exactly what happened. We were in our prayer circle in the living room, and the Holy Spirit moved and His power came upon us all. When the Spirit moves, we move, and we don't take His anointing lightly. This is in line with Ephesians 3:20, which says, "Now to him who is able to do immeasurably more than all we ask or imagine, according to his power that is at work within us." This verse describes how God's power enables us to do things that are impossible on our own, such as overcoming sin and speaking about Jesus Christ. After I reminded Bonita of the prophetic word, she said, "It's been so long that I almost forgot." From that day forward, we started making plans.

The Beginning Establishment

JEWELS IN HIS CROWN

"The Lord their God will save his people
on that day as a shepherd saves his flock.
They will sparkle in his land like jewels in
a crown" (Zechariah 9:16).

Jewels are precious stones that are highly esteemed, also known as precious gems. We are God's display of love and kindness. We belong to Him, the Father of the Lord Jesus Christ. We represent the value and importance of God's people. We are cherished and highly regarded by the Father. God's deliverance takes place in each individual, because we are restored as we sparkle in His land like Jewels in His crown. His righteous hand is on all of us individually and sometimes as a whole. God's plans are to prosper and protect us. Malachi 3:17 reads, "They will be my treasured possession." It is a sure reward from our Father to be honored in this special way. We have accepted the challenge to be Jewels in His crown. We pay a higher price to be a Jewel. We are a beautiful fit in His crown. In order to be the perfect fit, it requires you to be righteous. You are called to be holy and set a part. He has chosen us from all the nations of earth to be His own special treasure (Deuteronomy 14:2).

Jewels for Grace (J4G) is a non-profit organization established in January 2021. The scripture that we stand on is Habakkuk 2:2: "Write down the revelation and make it plain." Our mission is to be led by the Holy Spirit. We follow God and harken to His voice while we uplift families. We inspire to create an environment of love, friendship, and support, all while sharing wisdom and encouraging families to be well grounded in the Lord Jesus Christ. We give freely of our time, funds, resources, gifts, businesses, and talents. We have a special heart for women. As we love and intercede for all, being a strong voice and strength for our women gives us so much joy.

Our Jewel Bonita Irby is our visionary, along with Jewel Lashone Strickland as co-visionary. Pastor Linda Anderson is our spiritual mother and covering. Pastor Linda works behind the scenes with her prayers and anything else that we need. She is the mother of our group. She takes care of us all. This is a great blessing to J4G. Before you can be great, you need someone that came before that was the greatest. God wants you to have faith. He will give you a glimpse or a small piece of the puzzle. He will never show you the complete puzzle. That requires you to have faith. Faith pleases our Father. Without faith, we don't please our Father.

When a person comes into your life, they will either add to you or take from you. The ones that add to you are the ones to keep around. They are surely those that God has designed for you. We have Jewel Daetanya Taylor, Jewel Dawn Page, and Jewel Carolyn Bates, who all joined the first year we were established. These Jewels have been so faithful to run with the vision. They are beautiful in the crown of God. They have the most humble and loving hearts ever. God knew exactly what He was doing when He called these three in particular. We have Daja Miller as a secretary for Jewels for Grace. She works behind the scenes for J4G. She gets everyone's information and pulls names. She keeps up with who got who names for the year. Jewels call her to get addresses, emails, etc. They also call her to deliver gifts to another Jewel as needed. Daja is the daughter of Jewel Bonita and niece of Jewel Lashone. She has kept our records in order year after year. She always answers with a smile and a willing heart to step in to help. We often randomly send her a surprise gift to show our appreciation in working behind the scenes.

When J4G first got started, we read books together as a group. We came together to discuss each chapter. We also pulled names and called this a Secret Sister. Once you get your sister's name in private, you send gifts through the mail with no name on the packages. This was done to keep the secret going, leaving a mystery puzzle for the Jewel to figure out. Gifts were sometimes sent on a random Tuesday, but they were also sent when it was a certain holiday like Valentine's or Mother's Day—and on birthdays, of course. As a group, we support one another in times of bereavement as well as in accomplishments. We do conference calls to pray or to discuss the next topic.

At the end of the year, we go out to dinner and bring gifts, and this is also when we do the big Secret Sister reveal. We love to play the game *Guess Who*. Surprisingly, most Jewels don't have a clue who had their name. No worries because Jewel Bonita always studies and watches to see who got who. Most of the time she is right. We all get a kick out of her really figuring out who got who. We use the app GroupMe for updates.

Every time we get a gift, we post pictures of what we received. This is just one example of how she figured out who had who. I am Jewel Lashone, and I love chocolate-covered strawberries. Of course I had some delivered to my Secret Sister. Well, Jewel Bonita knows that, so she took note of it. The next time I sent my Secret Sister a gift, it was a purse. She knows I love purses. She put two and two together, and she was right. Another example is how Jewel Dawn loves the brand Adidas, and she kept buying her Secret Sister Adidas. Jewel Bonita is always taking notes. We all really love this and can't wait to hear her story and how she figured this out before the Jewel even knows. Jewel Bonita knew before you knew.

This was a very fun and exciting year to start Jewels for Grace. We didn't realize that we would grow differently but better. This was just the first season of Jewels for Grace. God sends a new and fresh wind every year. All of this happened because we had the best example set in front of us with Pastor Linda. We loved and wanted it. What is on the head flows down. We desired this and heard from God and began to move. God will give you the desires of your heart. This is designed by God. It's all for the Kingdom and glory of God.

YEAR 2022

God is always talking, and we are listening. Nothing is meant to stay the same. We have to start somewhere. When you are healthy you are growing, God always has a different and better plan than what we have. We are just blessed to have an open door, a line of communication with the Father in Heaven to be obedient for His will. We didn't start perfectly, but we grew in His grace and mercy. It is a true gift and blessing for God to meet you where you are at. God put His power upon us and watched us manifest what He already planned for us. God will never force Himself on anyone. It's always your free will. The God we serve stays the same and waits on us to get it right. This is called mercy. Read Matthew 5:7: "Blessed are the merciful, for they will be shown mercy."

This was the year we invited Jewel Angela Geter and Jewel Reschelle Means. These two Jewels brought so much love and spice. God knew what He was doing. They accepted the invitation and fit right into His crown. We did the same things as 2021 but more of it. We prayed more and still completed reading books. We say something almost daily on GroupMe. At one point there were so many messages that Jewel

Reschelle said she would have to turn off her notifi-
cations. We were talking a lot on the threads during
the day, and her phone was alerting her all day, and
her nerves couldn't take it. We got the Holy Spirit
often, and when one person started in the chat, it
would often be going all day back-to-back. It's all love,
though, coming from Jewel Reschelle. We understood
her feelings on this. What we love about her is she
keeps it real. She said, "I will jump in sometimes with
y'all but not every day all day" (laugh out loud). We
would often go deep into our feelings, but not everyone would be on the chat at the same time. For in-
stance, Jewel Carolyn would get off work at a different
time than the rest of us, and we would already have
long paragraphs in the chat. So when Carolyn jumped
in on the conversation, it would start right back up
again. We had the best conversations, but I think we
have toned it down since then.

We were all so excited about our group. We laughed,
cried, and prayed together, but most importantly we
just loved Jesus and one another. Jewel Reschelle
made us laugh often. We loved that and we needed
that so much. It was a vital part of our ministry. If you
want to live longer, you should laugh often. Jewels for
Grace absolutely loved our new voices, Jewel Angela

and Jewel Reschelle. These two were a blessing for our group. They love and cherish God just as we do. Jewel Angela brought such a sweet and loving spirit. She has the voice of an angel. This was a perfect combination designed by God. Everyone loved and accepted these two new shining Jewels. It's just like God to give you a precious gift that you didn't know you needed. Even though the Jewels were more in number and thus had more varieties in the Secret Sisters, it didn't matter because Jewel Bonita still studied and watched. She figured out who had who again. The new gifts that Jewel Angie and Jewel Reschelle sent out looked different than the ones that went out last year. Laugh out loud, because Bonita is putting together the mystery puzzle. When we got together for our end of the year Christmas Secret Sister reveal, Bonita was mostly right on about who had who. We enjoyed another great year with J4G. Thanking God for adding more Jewels in His crown.

Year 2022/2023

As we entered a new year, it was clear that God was speaking to us. We are always grateful and thankful to be in His will. You know the saying *the more the merrier*. That's exactly what happened. We invited Jewel Lisa Moore in November of 2022 and Jewel Mary Keels in February of 2023, and they both graciously accepted our invitation. We could tell that this would be a year of fresh wind, and a lot would change. Jewels for Grace grew so much that year. We had our first photo shoot with the girls in the new year, and we got our first J4G t-shirt designed with our names on the shirts. We had a beautiful gathering, and of course we had food and games to play. It's never a dull moment with these beauties. We always come and brighten the room with much love and laughter.

This was also the year J4G got a Facebook and Instagram account. This was a new and creative way to share our group, and we now post all our business plans and ideas on the sites. In this year of J4G, we honored Black History Month, Women's Month, Mother's Day, Father's Day, Birthdays, and so much more. This was the year that we introduced each Jewel, and a picture of them along with a short biography was introduced on Facebook, describing who they are and what perfection is and minimum information on their everyday life. This was a great way to introduce our group to the public. We followed that up by playing Thursday Trivia, where we asked a question to our Facebook followers about a Jewel. We then paid the first follower to get it right a cash prize. We had quite a few anonymous sisters, and this meant that a Jewel was randomly blessing another Jewel.

Jewels blessing other Jewels is done a lot in our group. One example is when Jewel Dawn came home from a long trip, and Jewel Lisa had gotten in her house and decorated it with a balloon arrangement, flowers, and a gift box full of her favorite things. Jewel Lisa did things like this quite often, and usually when a Jewel saw the unique package, they would say, "That ain't nobody but Lisa!" They were right because she is so anointed and gifted at everything that she does. That's what being a Jewel is all about. We are different and have different gifts. God blends them all together. Oh what a beautiful crown of Jewels we are, with His power, might, strength, and anointing in us. Greater is He that's in us than He that's in the world. We praise God for this.

This was also the year we came up with teams to help organize and build our group. We had so much fun creating these groups, and they are highlighted below.

The Visionaries

A visionary is a willing vessel that is given dreams and visions by the Lord. She adds the final pieces to the puzzle. She brainstorms in the middle of the night. She goes before Him early in her mornings. She steps up and becomes a visionary leader.

Her mission is to promise to show and demonstrate the greatest effort while giving beautiful meaning to life.

Her vision is to always have open minds to hear from God. We will not limit ourselves to our own thoughts and ideas, but to be open to His power, glory, and Holy Spirit.

Her purpose is to be an inspiration and encouragement for women and other individuals, creating an environment on how success looks and feels and letting His light shine.

"Then the Lord replied: Write down the revelation and make it plain upon tablets, so that a herald may run with it" (Habakkuk 2:2).

The Visionaries of Jewels for Grace are Jewel Bonita Irby and Jewel Lashone Strickland, blood sisters who are twins in spirit.

The Administrative Team

This Administrative Team plans, organizes, budgets, and creates ideas.

Their mission is to communicate new ideas, organize projects, bookkeep, research resources, and enhance wealth.

Their vision is to oversee all departments and to help with the balance and growth of all groups to be a success.

Their purpose is to create a positive non-profit organization that runs smoothly while being flexible and accountable in making decisions.

"But everything should be done in a fitting and orderly way" (1 Corinthians 14:40).

The Administrative Team includes Jewel Bonita Irby, Jewel Lashone Strickland, and Jewel Lisa Moore, who keep all things organized and ready.

The Prayer Team

This team comes to God through Jesus Christ without ceasing, both individually and jointly.

Their mission is to intercede to God constantly on behalf of others.

Their vision is to release God's love and power toward those who desire prayers for blessings, strength, encouragement, and comfort.

Their purpose is to be led by the Holy Spirit to bring all things back to Him and through Him.

"Rejoice always, pray continually, give thanks in all circumstances; for this is God's will for you in Christ Jesus" (1 Thessalonians 5:16-18).

The Prayer Team includes the following prayer warriors: Jewel Bonita Irby, Jewel Lashone Strickland, Jewel Carolyn Bates, Jewel Reschelle Means, and Jewel Lisa Moore. We keep prayer in everything we do.

The Financial Team

The Financial Team manages all aspects of the organization's financial health, working to build true financial freedom and wealth.

Their mission is to be a highly effective team that strives in business decisions to build our financial thinking and growth for success.

Their vision is to bless individuals accordingly and to help lead them to financial independence and freedom.

Their purpose is to have a healthy business mindset, growing in wealth and creating successful business opportunities. The secret to wealth for this group is to simply find a way to do more for others than anyone else does.

"But remember the Lord your God, for it is he who gives you the ability to produce wealth, and so confirms his covenant, which he swore to your ancestors, as it is today" (Deuteronomy 8:18).

The Financial Team includes Jewel Bonita Irby, Jewel Lashone Strickland, Jewel Daetanya Taylor, Jewel Angela Geter, and Jewel Lisa Moore. Wealth and riches shall be in our house.

The Celebration Team

The Celebration Team recognizes and celebrates everyone. They organize, create, and plan for individuals. They create birthday themes and gatherings for all types of special occasions.

Their mission is to celebrate and give recognition and honor to individuals on their special day.

Their vision to deepen the bond and heart for one another, building a lifetime of appreciation and gratitude.

Their purpose is to show and give love often, to give roses when it matters, and to appreciate and honor individuals on special occasions.

"Rejoice in the Lord always. I will say it again: Rejoice! Let your gentleness be evident to all. The Lord is near. Do not be anxious about anything, but in every situation, by prayer and petition, with thanksgiving, present your requests to God. And the peace of God, which transcends all understanding, will guard your hearts and your minds in Christ Jesus" (Philippians 4:4-7).

The Celebration Team includes Jewel Lisa Moore, Jewel Daetanya Taylor, and Jewel Mary Keels. Love never fails where we live today!

The Image Team

The Image Team captures images and videos for all events, which includes preparing the proper lighting and props for beautiful photos.

Their mission is to tell a story with their lenses by capturing the most precious moments in a single shot.

Their vision is to create memories for a lifetime to come by having an artistic vision and letting their hearts and minds flow freely with creativity.

Their purpose is to captivate the art of beauty.

"I praise you because I am fearfully and wonderfully made; your works are wonderful, I know that full well" (Psalms 139:14).

The Image Team includes Jewel Reschelle Means and Jewel Dawn Page, who help share cherished memories.

The Special Occasion Team

The Special Occasion Team honors people with crowns, birthday pins, satchels, corsages, jewelry, and ribbons.

Their mission is to maximize the enjoyment of individuals on special occasions, such as birthdays, anniversaries, weddings, baby showers, bridal showers, and all other celebratory events and occasions.

Their vision is to customize each individual with some sort of beautiful and expressive unique accessory or designed assortment.

Their purpose is to personalize each individual with a unique and distinctive design for any special occasion or event.

"You will be a crown of splendor in the Lord's hand, a royal diadem in the hand of you God" (Isaiah 62:3).

The Special Occasion Team includes Jewel Dawn A. Page, Jewel Reschelle Means, and Jewel Carolyn Bates, who are all pure-hearted and sweet women.

The Caregiver Team

The Caregiver Team are comfort keepers that elevate the human spirit for behind-the-scenes helpers or volunteers for Jewels for Grace.

Their mission is to shower individuals with unlimited love and gifts, as is shown in 1 Corinthians 13:4: "Love is patient, love is kind."

Their vision is to uplift individuals by surprise, making them know and feel the precious love of God through different gestures.

Their purpose is to show and demonstrate the true meaning of Jewels for Grace.

"My commandment is this: Love each other as I have loved you" (John 15:12).

The Caregiver Team includes Jewel Dawn Page and Jewel Carolyn Bates, or better known as Ms. Invincible (Dawn) and Ms. Authentic (Carolyn).

The Design Team

The Design Team creates a look for Jewels for Grace. Fashion fades, but style is eternal. Style is a way of saying who you are without having to speak. This team creates clothing that is customized from their own designs. They also market ready-to-wear clothing.

Their mission is to style Jewels for Grace in high fashion specifically designed by the Design Team. They pull from ready-to-wear clothing as well to edify and accommodate each Jewel.

Their vision is to unify and create a complete and captivating look in unity and oneness.

Their purpose is to complement our group by encouraging individuals to have a unique identity and to create an expression of art in exquisite detail and taste.

"She is clothed with strength and dignity; she can laugh at the days to come" (Psalms 31:25).

The Design Team consists of Jewel Lashone Strickland.

This is the demonstration of all of us being gifted. We use our gifts and put them together. We make a beautiful team.

2023 was also the year that we started to give back to the community. In order to do this, we needed money. So we started to really put the word out of who we are and what all we do on Facebook and Instagram. We did pocketbook raffles where we gave away beautiful purses that women really love. We would do a live drawing on our Facebook page for the purses, and then we would also give the second and third place winners a monetary gift. Everyone loves to win and to get on our Facebook page. It is quite an honor and blessing to be recognized. We also sold candles to raise money, and we used the money from our fundraisers to bless our graduates with a reward for all their hard work. They graduated high school with honors by maintaining a high GPA. We had our very own Jewel Carolyn's granddaughter graduate college with outstanding achievements. We love to celebrate our youth and give them the encouragement to keep going. We understand it's not easy and it takes discipline to finish your assignments.

At the end of the year, we had our first Christmas giveaway. J4G gave to the center for children. Each child wrote a wish list that we could fulfill. It was such a pleasure and a joy to put smiles on the children's faces while fulfilling their wishes on the day that we celebrate Jesus' birthday. Another giveaway was we randomly picked a Walmart Christmas shopper. The lady had twin boys, and she ended up with a buggy full of toys. The love of Jesus was shown. This is what it is all about: we give glory to God. That same day we went to the grocery store. There was a lady in the store that got blessed unexpectedly by J4G. The look on their faces was everything.

We feel like we are getting just as blessed as them simply by viewing their reactions. This is a great way to be a witness through the act of kindness. People's hearts are open to receive. Our focus is to show Jesus and demonstrate His pure love. The world we live in is full of darkness. His children are called to be His light. We are merely the light in His crown. Our connection through the source brings light, love, and kindness. We know that this is the will of God because it's His Word. His Word stands forever. Nothing in the natural world is forever; everything changes. We go through four seasons a year, and the summer of 2020 was different from the summer of 2024. But God stays the same and He can't lie. We are here to practice being a saint. What you do on this earth will determine if you make it to be a saint in heaven. Practice brings perfection and that brings protection. Storms will come, but they are designed to make you stronger. In the midst of it, He will not take His righteous hands off of you. It is an absolute honor to be Jewels in His crown. We study, pray, fast, laugh, cry, have fun, and bless people. Every year we become shinier and shinier. Being polished by the King takes time, obedience, and discipline. It's not easy, and we are not perfect. We repent of our sins because "all have sinned and fall short of the glory of God" (Romans 3:23).

Throughout the year, we made sure to celebrate everyone's birthday. We would go out to a restaurant or to a party celebrating a Jewel. Jewel Lisa led the celebration committee team. This was such a beautiful set up designed by Jewel Lisa. She spent hours and hours decorating for a Jewel's birthday. She designed it with lavish colors and a special theme according to the style of the particular Jewel. She did an exquisite job for Jewel Daetanya's fiftieth birthday celebration. The color she led with was purple, the color of royalty. What a beautiful sight to see. God has blessed

Jewel Lisa with the gift to decorate. This is one of many gifts that she blessed our group with. She is an event planner that is exceptionally blessed with the most creative ideas. Jewel Daetanya's celebration was a fun time for all of us to be a part of. We had good food, such as crab legs, shrimp, fish, and chicken, and the husbands of Jewels for Grace—Tony, Mark, and Garnell—served us. It was a precious and selfless thing for these men to do. They did this twice in the summer of 2023. J4G honors these three for showing up for us. We don't take it for granted. They even helped move furniture into a young lady's apartment. We had three trucks filled with furniture. God is better than good for the act of kindness, love, and light to show up in the husbands of Jewels for Grace. It takes a special kind. Everything we do is for the glory of God. Yielding to Him is being an example of Christ.

Year 2024

2024 was the year for more and more and more. More of God's supernatural strength and wisdom. We believe and receive all upgrades in our life that's to come. "Write down the revelation and make it plain on tablets so that a herald may run with it" (Habakkuk 2:2). This is one of J4G's favorite scriptures, one of many. 2024 was the year that we first came together and created our vision board. We have plans that we would love to see manifest. One thing is to have a safe haven for women. This would be a home for women to come and stay until they can get a job or a safe place to stay. This facility would be open for their children as well. We would offer free food and clothing, and we would have the resources to help them find jobs. We would also give them a complete makeover—from hair to skin care—getting them ready for their glamour shots. Everyone needs a headshot for business. We aim to make them beautiful and put a smile on their faces. We plan to have affordable housing. "She opens her arms to the poor and extends her hands to the needy. When it snows, she has no fear for her household; for all of them are clothed in scarlet" (Proverbs 31:20-21). It is power in purpose. Our greatest purpose is to serve and to show compassion and love to others. Empowered women empower women often and on time.

WOMEN'S HISTORY MONTH
MARCH 2024

If you are a woman of God full of grace, if you are a family woman, if you are a businesswoman, or if you are connected to J4G in any way, then March is the month that we acknowledge you on our Facebook page. J4G loves to uplift and inspire women to be more than what they already are. There is always more inside of you that you haven't discovered yet. One example of what we did was that we wrote a small biography about several great women of God, and they only knew when they were tagged on Facebook. We already know the great feeling you get by simply being a blessing to others, so it was our honor to surprise these women of God with a picture of them and a biography about their life, accomplishments, and character.

This was also the month that the J4G marched. This is called a Jericho March. The power of God showed up. Our spiritual mom, Pastor Linda, led this march. The Jewels got in their cars along with Pastor Linda and drove to each Jewel house. We then got out of our cars and marched around each Jewel house seven times. While marching, the prayers were going up.

They decreed and declared the Word and blessings of God over their life. When we pray, we pray to the will of God. The anointing was there, and angels were released on assignment to fight. These ladies came for war in their army uniforms and colors. Don't let that fool you, we didn't come to be cute. It was with unity and one accord. The Jewels live in different cities upstate, so we were driving from Piedmont, stopping in Greer, and heading to Spartanburg. We were on a mission, and it got done. The walls fell down, and some Jewels got a breakthrough.

When you fight in the Spirit, big changes come. This is the Lord's army. "Whatever you bind on earth will be bound in heaven, and whatever you loose on earth will be loosed in heaven" (Mathew 18:18). Victory is ours through Christ Jesus. The Jewels were true warriors on that day of March. They marched in miracles. We put others first and saw what God did. We didn't see that coming. Blessings that just pop up are the best kind. Your obedience is always better than a sacrifice. Obeying God lets Him know He can trust you. This keeps you in the will of God.

Resurrection Sunday came in March this year. Many say that it was early, but the God we serve is always on time. This is a month for miracles to come to pass and to give. God gave the best gift to be given. He gave His only begotten Son, Jesus Christ. We could never repay Him for that. The goal is to serve, honor, obey, worship, and praise Him. This is the best way to invest your heart and time. Be truthful and always repent and confess your sins. Always forgive your neighbor or enemies. This is the only way to get your prayers answered and for God to forgive you. God has used His Word to transform us into women of divine power who reflect His beauty. Jewels for Grace isn't just a name. God displays us in whatever light He wants to. It takes obedience to be in His will. It's not easy but a call from Him. His Holy Spirit has the power and anointing to get you through. Start praising Him in advance, no matter what it looks like. It's impossible to please God without faith. We are His willing vessels. His creation works for all of us, creating the most creative and unique style. He displays us as powerful and wealthy daughters of God. We are called to reach nations, and we are handpicked by the Father to be Jewels in His crown.

The month of May is so dear to our hearts, as it is the month when we honor all of the Jewels for Grace mothers on our Facebook page. We put their picture up and write about them. We make sure we honor these mothers, even if they are simply a mother to their nieces and nephews or to their godchildren. Mothers come in so many different ways. A mother is not always blood or biological. A mother is a woman that is good to her children. She is the reason so many feel loved. She is the connection that the children need. A mother's touch is gentle. A mother's love is forever. A mother knows just how much is needed. She can look at you and see so much. She knows your present by looking at you. She doesn't judge you for your past. She helps you grow through it. She is a woman who God has especially for you. That doesn't necessarily mean she birthed you, but most times this is true. Everyone knows you don't mess with a mama's baby bear. Women are protective over their children in more than one way. One additional note: because we don't live in a perfect world, some people don't have moms that fit the above description. In these cases, the God we serve has women lined up to be a mother to a motherless child.

Speaking to all women, God made you differently. He trusted us to carry the seed of the baby. A man planted the seed, but He trusted a woman to carry the plan of the unborn child. He chose us, and God didn't make any mistakes. He knows the specific needs of children. Children need love and nurture, and we are naturally designed that way. Men have other qualities that women don't. It goes together. There is a certain level of discipline that a man can give to his children that's needed from a man's role. Women can also provide discipline because we are so versatile, but the male authority says something different. When my grandfather walked into the room, everyone got quiet. He was a good gentleman who didn't let anyone mess with his family. If I consider my own family, being a mother of three sons, the role their dad plays is very much needed. His voice is needed to stand behind my voice. He is a stronger discipliner than I am. Dads' relationships with their daughters are unique—just think of the daddy's girls—but the mom has something more to give when it comes to girl things. When a girl's body changes, she needs her mother.

Women, my hat goes off to those of you who don't have help from their husband, dad, brother, or uncle. Being a husband and father are two different things. Men that can conquer being a husband and a father have to be led by God. This isn't an easy task. You do have some that can't be a husband and end up being a great father. When they can do both, that is a double blessing. God honors that and will favor you. J4G loves families and prays that the blessings of the Lord stay upon them. "Commit to the Lord whatever you do, and He will establish your plans" (Proverbs 16:3).

Let's Pray together . . .

Father God, we humbly come before your throne of grace. We first ask for forgiveness of our sins. We repent of wrong thinking and small thinking. We renounce the old covenant of bad thoughts. We ask for a new covenant of blessings with a new mind complete in you. We think positive and act brand new in Christ Jesus. The Lord teaches us how to be great women of God. With that we are great to our families and other women around us. Show us how to be a woman of great value for your Kingdom. We pray to have a forever heart and desire to bless your children, our brothers and sisters in Christ. May the woman reading this book confess that she is a daughter of the King. I pray that she dedicates her life and soul to you. Romans 10:9 says, "If you declare with your mouth, 'Jesus is Lord,' and believe in your heart that God raised him from the dead, you will be saved." Thank you, Father, for saving your precious daughter. Let your Word that's within her shine like never before with a God glow. In Jesus' holy name. Amen.

May Graduation

May is not only the month to celebrate mothers. It's also graduation time for our youth. It's our biggest joy to have a hand in the journey of a young adult's life. We chose a very gifted young man to give a college scholarship to this year. We posted graduation pictures and wrote a list of accomplishments for the graduate on our Facebook page, such as GPA, sports, jobs, and volunteer time. Jewel Lashone even had a tribute for the graduate. This took place at his graduation party with family and friends. The graduate has so many great qualities, such as wisdom, power, longevity, stability, endurance, resilience, and honesty, so the illustration that Jewel Lashone gave was of the acorn seed. Let me go in detail about the meaning of the acorn seed.

The acorn is a symbol of growth and unlimited potential. The acorn contains a very sacred seed. The acorn produces the seed of the mighty oak tree, which is a symbol of wisdom. The oak tree is the tree of life. It is the largest, strongest, and longest living tree of all trees. This tree of knowledge lives a life span of thousands of years, and it only takes one acorn to grow this tree. God spoke this illustration over this young man's life. He is oak strong and ready for the adventure of life. Jewel Lashone left him with the scripture of Isaiah 61:3: "To bestow on them a crown of beauty instead of ashes, the oil of joy instead of mourning, and a garment of praise instead of a spirit of despair. They will be called oaks of righteousness, a planting of the Lord for the display of his splendor."

God loves His little children and loves when they are raised in Him, and He trusts his mother to carry out the plans. Well done, good and faithful servant. My advice to you is to raise your children with the Spirit of God. Always obey and hear instructions for your child. Know that each child is different and that you have to go to the Father for a plan. It takes self-discipline to be a good parent. To be a great parent it's going to be a sacrifice. You need the Father to guide and protect you. This temporary world we live in is set up to try and destroy your children. As a parent, your job is to stop evil from destroying your seeds. Not all are given the opportunity to plant a seed of an acorn. As long as you have the seed to plant, plant your seed in good soil, and water your seed. Pray over your seed and protect your seed. You have nourishment that you get from the Father.

It should be easy to give back to your children, but I hear so many adults say that they didn't get nourished by their parents, which took away a loving nature that should be natural. It made them very hard and selfish. For example, I hear some adults say that they had to work to buy their first car—no one helped them—so their kids should have to buy their own as well. In contrast, our family tradition is to buy the teenager their first car. I say do what feels right and not what someone has done to you.

There are many different ways to show your kids responsibilities, but only if your kid is responsible enough in your eyes. It takes parents to raise them and to start training early, giving them a great foundation. I believe once you give your children a head start, you are setting them up for a bright future. This is starting a generational covenant and blessing for your family. The best gift you can give to your seeds is a love that shows nothing but love. I know what was done to me, both right and wrong. My best decision is to do what is right, and not only that, but what feels right. Love your children with the love of God. There will always be a time of correction and even punishment. They need to be held accountable for their actions. But they will grow through their mistakes, so coach them through these experiences in life. Being a parent is a full-time job. It makes a difference in your child's life and wellbeing. Take time to learn about your children, because each one is different and may require something different from their siblings. Learn their love language, as some might need affirmations and words of encouragement. This is a blessing for our families all over the world. It also brings order and balance. Harmony is our goal, not what your parents did to you. Don't pick up neglectful behavior or patterns. This is the ultimate goal of goals.

Support

J4G supports all of our sisters through all life's challenges. We celebrate as the occasion comes up. One of our favorite celebrations in 2024 was Jewel Reschelle being fourteen years cancer-free. God is better than good. She went from a survivor to an overcomer and now a warrior. J4G is honored to have this special lady of the Lord as a shining Jewel. God has blessed her with uncommon favor. She gives her heart to the Jewels. She is a true guiding light in this world. She is a strong warrior. To God be the glory.

J4G Annual Secret Sister Christmas Gathering!

On the first of the month of December, we took the time to love and celebrate one another. We revealed who our Secret Sisters were for the year. We also shared our plans and vision for the upcoming year.

We are so grateful for the partnership with one another that is rooted through Christ Jesus. To watch us grow over the years has been a great blessing. Our mission is to build each other up while we build the community up around us. Job 8:7 says, "Your beginnings will seem humble, so prosperous will your future be." We are honored to be Jewels in His crown.

Christmas Giveaways 2024

Jewels for Grace had a blessed opportunity to serve at the Ronald McDonald House at the end of 2024. The Ronald McDonald House is a non-profit family and children charity dedicated to supporting families with children in their time of need during medical care. This organization is located in Greenville, South Carolina. We came together, purchased food, and cooked meals for families. The Ronald McDonald House has a kitchen and cooking utensils on site. This made things much better for cooking. There was no hauling food around since everything was in one place. During seasons of giving like these, we want to express how important it is to serve with all of your heart, your time, and your energy. We absolutely love what we do. When our vision and mission come to pass, it demonstrates the light of the Lord. Glory to God!

"May your deeds be shown to your servants, your splendor to their children. May the favor of the Lord our God rest on us; establish the work of our hands for us—yes, establish the work of our hands" (Psalm 90:16-17).

Another Christmas giveaway that we created was blankets for the homeless. Our hearts overflowed with joy. This was an incredible experience to witness. We were blessed with enough blankets to stop at three different charities for children, women, and men. Belle Realty and Associates, a real estate company that Jewel Reschelle is a partner at, along with Carolina Style Hair Salon and The Slaughterhouse Salon, generously set up a drop-off location for the blankets. The community really got involved and did a great service to help our families in need. Upstate Greenville came together to be a blessing, and the blanket drive was a success. Having a servant's heart is the best gift you can give.

2025 Alive and Revived

2025 is the year of transformation and renewal! We have great expectations for this year, and we started out the year with the Jewels For Grace Purified By Fire Ceremony! Our spiritual mom, Pastor Linda, was with us as we had our service, and Jewel Reschelle taught a powerful word on purity and getting rid of all the evil and negativity that's in our hearts. She went into great detail, and the room was so quiet that you could hear a pin drop. We all received the word she delivered. We knew she spent time with the Father to deliver this word. We had on all-white clothing, with no makeup or jewelry—only a wedding band was permitted, if married. Then we had a lighting of the candles, which was a symbol of our vow to God. This was truly a blessing. We were purified by His anointing and grace. We took communion and worshiped the Lord God Almighty. This was the absolute best way to start our new year.

JUNIOR JEWELS

Every year things change for the better. This year we got a surprise, and we grew in a different and major way. God added five Junior Jewels and one Junior Jewel in training. These young ladies are eighteen to thirty-five years of age and are just starting their walk with the Father as an adult daughter of God. They are so excited and hungry for the Word. They love God with all their hearts, and they are looking for a spiritual mentor—someone who has been walking with the Lord for a while. They want to be around the fire of God. The light that's in us transfers into them. The deeper you grow in Him, the stronger and brighter your light gets. God has raised us up to be Naomis to these Ruths. They are called unto God to be a daughter of God. God sees them as Jewels in His creation. He is molding them and making them the way He wants them to be designed.

Introducing the Junior Jewels

The first to be introduced is Junior Jewel Daja Miller, who is the daughter of Jewel Bonita. Daja started out four years ago as our behind-the-scenes secretary. She has been around the fire, and she knew exactly what she was getting into. She loves the bond that we share and the love and support we have for one another, as well as our giving to organizations and individuals. Daja has a beautiful daughter who she cherishes. She is also an anointed praise dancer, which she has been doing since she was a young girl.

The next Junior Jewel we have is Jasmine Taylor, who is the daughter-in-law of Jewel Daetanya. Junior Jewel Jasmine was inspired by her mother-in-law in all the different things that she was involved in. Her desire is God, so it makes it easy for her to be a Junior Jewel. Jasmine is a wife, and a mother to her son. Jasmine is also a licensed nurse (LPN). She has a heart for people. Follow her on TikTok and Instagram to see some of her some amazing videos.

Next, we have two Junior Jewels, namely Jewel Mady Tribble and Jewel Hanna Tribble, who are sisters. Junior Jewel Mady is a friend of Jewel Reschelle, who has become a mentor to Mady. Real estate is what brought these two together, and then Junior Jewel Mady shared with her sister what she was witnessing. These two remind me of how Jewel Bonita and I were when we were younger. They are quiet but loving. They stick together and have a lovely sister bond. I can't wait to see what God is going to do with these two, both in the spirit and naturally. Junior Jewel Mady is in real estate school, and I'm convinced she will become a top-selling realtor. Jewel Hanna Tribble is studying to become a nurse. Hanna loves her precious daughter and enjoys spending time with her. Their relationship is a sweet blessing. These sisters love God and want more of Him.

Then we have Junior Jewel Mia Jenkins, who is the niece of Jewel Bonita. She is very passionate about the things of God, and is hungry for the Word of God. She has a beautiful heart and soul. She is building herself up stronger and stronger, and she is super blessed. God will indeed make all things new for her. Mia has two adorable daughters, and she is an amazing mom to these girls. Mia is a licensed esthetician. She does amazing work.

Next, we have Junior Jewel Angel, who is in training to be a Junior Jewel. She is the daughter of Jewel Bonita. She has been around the fire for a while, watching and watching. She is growing into a fine young lady. When it comes to God, it is never too early. We are so proud of this young lady. She has the perfect name, which means messenger. To be a messenger of God is an honor. He can trust you in His presence. Glory be to God. Angel is the youngest of four siblings, she is a cheerleader for her school, and she loves to praise dance. The anointing is with her. Her parents are very supportive and proud of Angel.

Daja and Angel are blood sisters, but they have an age gap. From my experience, God has shown that He has His own special timing, and this sister bond and relationship will grow into the same bond and relationship that their mom and I have. It's beautiful for us to see. Power is in the sister's unity and love. God is with them in all that they do. Their latter days will be greater. They often praise dance together. They are an anointed and powerful duo. All praises to God!

We love all our Junior Jewels wholeheartedly. Our mission is to help these young ladies grow in the Kingdom of God, to mentor them while they excel in their personal life as well as their spiritual life, and to instill inside of them all the values that have already been instilled in us. Overall, we want to be an all-around complete blessing to these young ladies. We walk by faith and not by sight. "As iron sharpens iron, so one person sharpens another" (Proverbs 27:17). We rely on the Holy Spirit to lead and guide us. This is our way to share wisdom and our past experiences with our Juniors. If you haven't lived, then what do you know? How can you advise me if you have always walked a straight and narrow path?

Moses taught Joshua how to lead Israel to the promised land. Elijah inspired and taught Elisha to eventually take over Elijah's ministry. We are Naomis to our Junior Jewels, and they are our Ruths. I recommend you to read the entire book of Ruth. It is a great love story. It's about being loyal and keeping your faith no matter what it looks like. Kindness and generosity bring life. Ruth made a vow to serve the God of Israel, and in so doing, made a personal sacrifice. She was a Moabite who converted to the faith of Israel. She didn't know that the decisions she made early on was going to get her favor with Boaz, who became her husband. She also didn't know she would be the great-grandmother of Jesus. Ruth's story is a beautiful example of how God can turn a broken situation into greatness. God has a plan for everyone and rewards faithfulness. Just like your job can promote or reward you, so can God. When God rewards you, no one can undo it. Think about what Ruth went through before she got her reward. Three men, three deaths, and three widows later . . . you can't tell me she didn't go through it. How many nights did she stay up grieving? Most of us would have a mental breakdown after the first time, but three times? That curse was broken because of her reaction to the hand she was given.

Your hand is your hand in spite of it being a bad game. Even when you keep losing the game, don't you ever give up. As long as you have breath, decide to fight. Your beginning is not more important than your ending. This builds character, strength, and determination. Pray for God to help put you in a position to be a mentor. There is someone for everyone. Ask Him to show you who. Build a relationship by starting off with prayer. Pray for the Holy Spirit to lead you. If you are reading this book and are looking for a Naomi, for someone to mentor you, then pray to our Father, and He will direct your path. When He orders your steps, you fall into the right places. Naomi's faith in God was incredibly strong. Ruth demonstrated faith, courage, and loyalty. Remember that what's in your heart will come out in your decisions. Just make sure you have the right feelings, emotions, and purities in your heart. The decisions you make will determine your future. Let's pray!

Dear Heavenly Father, we praise your holy name for revelation and understanding. We praise you for exactly who you are in our life. You are Lord God Almighty in our lives. Let our past be our past. May we live in our present. Forgive us our daily sins, knowing and unknowing. Please wash us in the blood of the Lamb. Purify our hearts and minds to be free from all curses. We renounce the spirit of bitterness, lack of control, stubbornness, jealousy, and rebellion. We ask for you to replace it with a new covenant of blessings filled with love, compassion, forgiveness, agreement, unity, loyalty, and honesty. Let your will be done. Raise your Naomis up to be what you have called and designed them to be. May they be willing vessels for their Ruths. We ask for divine connections with the mentors and mentees, and a sweet anointing and protection for their relationship. We pray for the relationship to grow and blossom into a beautiful friendship. We ask for your great divine favor, mercy, grace, and protection to be upon us. We ask for your blessing, Father. We confess to walk in love and light. We confess to be true to you and have faith that no matter the obstacle, the great reward will be on the other side. We confess not to give up and to place all our faith in you Lord Jesus. We confess that today is a new day. We will honor you all the days of our lives. We confess to getting spiritually fit daily. We love and honor you, King Jesus. We seal our prayers in the blood of Jesus. We ask this in Jesus' name.

SPIRITUALLY FIT

Being spiritually fit means to be in shape in the spirit realm. We live in a spiritual world. Our job is to fight. The enemy is looking for a way to get you into bondage. If he gets your husband, the family is off. The main role for a man is a leadership role. If he is out of order, the family is out of order. If there is no order, then there is no balance in our lives. If the parents are in agreement with each other, the enemy will try and come through the kids. He has tricks, but it's not anything that the Holy Spirit can't warn you about. Listen to His voice. It's real and will be your best friend if you receive it.

Let's pause for a minute. If you are not already a born-again believer, invite the Holy Spirit to come live inside of you. Welcome Him, receive Him, and thank Him. You will want to invite Him daily, along with the inside of your home. When Jesus went home to be with the Father, He left us the gift of the Holy Spirit—the Holy Trinity, Father, Son, and Holy Spirit.

Don't second guess it. We don't need to focus on His plans and plots. Our goal is to get spiritually fit and fight for our families. Pray the Word of God with the authority God has given His children. Anoint your oil and pray over it and use it daily if you need it. Anoint your windows, doors, and every room in your home. Anoint your families and confess the Word of God over them. Find a scripture, and believe God for it. Stand on it until it comes to pass.

The next tool God has given us is to fast when you pray. Fasting goes along with prayer. "But when you fast, put oil on your head and wash your face, so that it will not be obvious to others that you are fasting, but only to your Father, who is unseen" (Matthew 6:16-18). You don't need to tell the world. The best thing you can do is get a fasting and praying partner. You will move mountains together in unity. There's so much power in agreement when two or more are together and believing in something. "Is not this the kind of fasting I have chosen: to loose the chains of injustice and untie the cords of the yoke, to set the oppressed free and break every yoke" (Isaiah 58). Fast with an open heart and hands to receive guidance from the Father. Repent of your sins and truly mean it. Humble yourself before God. Desire and look for a deeper spiritual connection with the Father. Have a willing heart and mind to receive God's presence. It is a beautiful gift to receive His love, mercy, and grace. Fasting brings discipline and kills the flesh. Fasting is refraining from all food except water. This brings spiritual clarity and purpose. During your fasting time, pray, praise, and worship. Amen, and thank you, Jesus.

Introduction of the Nine Jewels in His Crown

We are Jewels in His crown, women of divine grace. What that means is that we are to demonstrate light and love at all times. We do what we do because of the love we have for our Father in Heaven. We are crowned to the core. This means that we roll up our sleeves at any time, planned or unplanned. We fast and pray so we can yield to Him and say no to our flesh.

We are not perfect women, but we are perfectly in His crown. We are covered with the radiant glow reflecting from our Father. It's the anointing He has given us. We go through things just like everyone else. The difference is we are daughters of the King. The glory of God shows up and shines through us. It takes you walking with God in the times no one is around. We are called to a higher standard of excellence to serve in our community. We assist individuals to achieve their highest potential in life. We give our time, money, and prayers to families or individuals that are in need of our assistance. We support and build relationships with women as we inspire them. We are a sacred group of women that connect and share with one another.

In our leadership roles, we are excited about building a strong team for Jesus. Everything we do is for His Kingdom and not our own benefit. We are happy to share our organization with others. We would love for other women or teams to get inspired about the work we have done. The community wins when the number of organizations increases. It's never about us, but it is important to tell our story.

Being a Jewel in His crown demonstrates the nature of our heart. Our love is giving, openly and freely, to anyone God sends us to, whether we know them or not. Our eyes are fixed upon the Lord. We do our complete best to honor Him and bring glory to His holy name. We love our Father with all our heart. This is the reason why we do what we do in Jesus' name.

Introducing Jewel #1

Bonita Irby

She is not a one-in-a-million kind of a girl. She is a once-in-a-lifetime kind of woman. Personified as a woman of God, she is considered the best or most important of her kind. She brings beauty and grace, a clear example of a particular quality. She adds life to the lifeless. The stars are winking in the night sky over Bonita. To be this high ranking in quality is one of a kind.

She is the Honey Queen Bee Mrs. Bonita Miller Irby! Bonita is the visionary of Jewels for Grace. Outside of J4G, she has been a process leader at BMW Manufacturing for the last twenty-five years, managing her own team of individuals. She is also the owner and operator of TMC Tax Services, where she has operated as a professional licensed tax preparer for the last fourteen years. Her services are tax planning, tax returns, debt counseling, and credit advisor. Additionally, Bonita is co-owner of Angels of Hearts LLC, which is a real estate investment company that has been established for twenty-one years. She also has been a regional manager life insurance agent.

Bonita has been serving families for fifteen years. She is knowledgeable and passionate about investing into families and making sure that they are educated in protecting their families. Bonita is co-owner of Back-Yard Venue, which is an independently owned business. The BackYard Venue is available for different party events (birthday parties, private intimate events, family gatherings, etc.). The building comes with a huge open patio deck for outside events. Bonita is the most organized host you will ever meet. She is extremely gifted at putting a crowd together. People always show up in record numbers. She is a magnet that's like glue.

Bonita loves the Lord with everything in her. She is a praise and worship dancer before the Lord. She is an intercessor prayer warrior. She is a dreamer and an interpreter of dreams, and she has many visions. She is a speaker and encouragement to all mankind. She is a natural giver, with a compassionate heart for people. Bonita also has an anointing in finances, which means money gravitates to her like a magnet. Bonita is a financial bookkeeper for ministries in the Upstate of South Carolina. Bonita is a natural born leader, a Leo Queen who is good at what she does. She always has the winning team. The best part about all of this is that she is humble. All of her goodness comes from the Lord, and we call this blessed. Bonita has been married for twenty years to Tony, and they have been blessed with five children and six grandchildren. She has a very tight bond with her mom, sisters, five play daughters, playmates BFF (c-train), Charlie's Three Angels besties, and her family. She is a people person and knows how to build a relationship. God calls this a personified woman. The name Bonita means beautiful, as well as virtuous and good. She is a Jewel that fits perfectly in His crown.

Introducing Jewel #2

Jewel Lashone Strickland

This woman of God is a full circle, vividly bright and shining like glitter that gleams. She is a radiant soul that shines from the inside. She is as rare as a sunflower in the desert, a hidden gem with a radiant heart of light.

The stunning Jewel Lashone Strickland is co-visionary of Jewels for Grace. Outside of J4G, Lashone has been a licensed cosmetologist for twenty years. She specializes in natural hair care, and she has been gifted with servicing a variety of clientele. Lashone has also been a Title 1 teacher for Greenville County School District for the last eight years. She educates and trains students in reading and math, helping build their confidence and equip them with skills in education. Lashone has also been a life insurance agent, showing individuals how to plan for their future. Lashone is co-owner with her husband Garnell Jr. of Let's Gooo Auto Sales of Greer, SC, which is a car auto dealership that has been in operation for twenty years. She manages bookkeeping and all accounting needs for the family-owned dealership. Lashone is also co-owner with Garnell Jr. of Land Lenders LLC, which is a real estate investment business that has been in operation for fifteen years. They invest in properties through leasing and selling. Additionally, Lashone is a personal stylist for women. She styles according to the personality of the client. She completely styles the hair and the appropriate attire and jewelry for the evening. Lashone was voted best dressed at Carolina College of Hair Design—quite the fashionista! Lashone also has a gift of home interior decorating and loves to shop and create beautiful spaces.

Lashone has loved the Lord since as long as she can remember. God has blessed her with the gift to minister in dance. She is an intercessory prayer warrior. Lashone is a writer, and her first book was *Becoming A Fivefold Madam.* She is a dreamer. God gives her visions. The spirit of discernment has been there since childhood. She will not fit in with the crowd. She has a heart for teenage girls, teaching them to love and value themselves. She has trained the youth in dancing before the Lord. Lashone has been married for twenty-four years to Garnell Jr., and God has blessed them with three sons and three grandchildren. Lashone is an excellent cook for her family. She has been crowned the macaroni queen of the family. Families and businesses from the upstate have always requested her macaroni and cheese dish. She has a very close bond with her mom, sisters, nieces, nephews, and family. Her home has always been a safe haven for the family. Lashone means "the one who shines." The name signifies brightness and radiance. God calls this golden heart of light a Jewel in His crown.

INTRODUCING JEWEL #3
JEWEL DAETANYA TAYLOR

She is rare because she is real! She is a first-rate version of herself instead of a second-rate version of somebody else. Daetanya has been a dedicated process lead at BMW for twenty-five years. She is an advocate for individuals in her group and a natural born leader. She is a voice for many people. Daetanya actively supports and promotes the interests of individuals. Daetanya is owner and business manager for Taylor Made Catering, which is a family business that has served the community for many years.

God has given Daetanya as a treasure to her family. She is so important and valued by her children, grandchildren, and family. Daetanya is a pillar for her family, which is most precious to God. Her family will always be her beginning and end. She is a great leader and teacher for her family. Daetanya is the most impressive woman you will ever meet. God smiles because she remains dedicated no matter what. She has an everlasting strength from within. She doesn't need the approval of men. She knows her worth is more than silver and gold. Daetanya has been married for thirty years to Mark, and God has blessed them with two children, two daughters-in-law, and three grandkids. She is a loyal friend who you can always depend on. Daetanya is loved and cherished by many and most of all by our Father in Heaven. The name Daetanya is likely a unique creation that remains humble and anonymous. You can't put a finger on her. She is well protected by the Father. God's grace and mercy follows her. He has specifically designed her to be a perfect Jewel in His crown.

INTRODUCING JEWEL #4
JEWEL DAWN PAGE

Be the woman who fixes another woman's crown without telling the world it was crooked, just like the invisible Dawn Page. Dawn was active for thirty-one years serving our country in the US Army Reserve. She has traveled the world and lived in many different states. She was trained well to serve and protect our country.

Dawn is also a licensed certified notary ready to service you. She has excelled in photography for many years. Additionally, Dawn is an amazing caregiver for the youth and elderly, and she has taken care of family members that needed special attention with their health. She excelled as a softball player, leading her team to many victories. Dawn was voted most friendliest at Carolina High School.

She loves everyone unconditionally. She would give anyone the shirt off her back—a true example of a real friend. Dawn is a lupus survivor, and her strength has proven that she is incapable of being defeated. God admires Dawn! He has always given her the sword of the Spirit—a true warrior of the Lord. Her love for God, family, and friends is forever. God has blessed her with a son and grandson, and she has many godchildren. Dawn is a natural born fighter, and she wins. Jewels for Grace has always admired Dawn for her unique and incredible kindness. She is the definition of the nine fruits of the Spirit. The name Dawn means the first appearance of light. She represents renewed hope, freshness, and the beginning of a new chapter. She perfectly fits in His crown.

Introducing Jewel #5

Jewel Carolyn Bates

A quality woman isn't defined by her social status, race, money, or nationality. She's defined by her heart, which describes the authentic Carolyn Bates. She owns and operates a Servant's Heart, which is a self-made independently owned business. She is serving clients in all areas of the Upstate of South Carolina. She also incorporates a management team in the marketing retail department.

Carolyn is dedicated to the Kingdom of God. God is her first love and always will be. She has an anointing that most wouldn't understand. Her very love for Jesus Christ has called to walk in a different place than most believers. She is called to a higher calling. It takes discipline, courage, obedience, sacrifice, and patience. Carolyn has danced before the Lord for many, many years. She is a true praise dancer for the Kingdom of God. She has been anointed for intercessory praying in the midnight hours. Whenever the Holy Spirit comes, she is ready. She is a speaker of the Word of God. She hears from God and is a mighty prophet that takes purity from God. She volunteers her time in the community. These are some of her favorite gifts of the ministry. Our Father in Heaven, her mother, daughter, and three grandchildren, and her family cherish and love Carolyn dearly. The name Carolyn means strong or free. She is perceived as trustworthy and capable. She values relationships and traditions. She serves as a cornerstone in her community. She is the apple of His eye that fits perfectly in His crown.

Introducing Jewel #6

Jewel Angela Geter

Pretty as an accident of nature and elegant as a self-created work of art, Angie has a light that sparks in her. In her own way, she illuminates the world. The illuminated and beautiful Angie Geter has been a licensed professional tax preparer for over seventeen years. She is the owner and CEO of JAG Tax Service Unlimited, and her services are tax planning, tax returns, payroll services, financial reports, debt counseling, and credit restoration. Angela helps new businesses get started with the needs of funding and helping build credit. She is a prosperity leader for many. She is knowledgeable and experienced with financial planning and all-around increases. Angie is owner of Capital Chic$, which focuses on individual teaching and training on how to build your credit in multiple ways. She has record breaking numbers when it comes to wealth management and helping you build your credit. Angela exceeds her strengths and abilities with knowledge used to serve the Upstate of South Carolina. She is a licensed legal binding notary. Angela has been married for thirty-two years to Jerome, and they have been blessed with three adult children that they love freely, as well as five grandchildren.

Angie is a faithful servant of the Lord. She has an anointed voice and has been singing melodies since a little girl—she has the voice of an angel. She has been a member of her church choir for most of her life. She is very active in the church, and is always coming up with strategies to bring to the youth to keep them more engaged in the community. Angela has an eye for fashion. She designs bows and socks for little girls. Angie loves to laugh and have a good time. Her smile and laugh are priceless. God smiles back at Angela and He cherishes her. She is a beacon of light that shines. She brings things to order, and it is clarifying. To illuminate is to be Angela, meaning she is a shining light with knowledge. She is the light of many souls. Her parents made no mistake when they named her Angela, which means angel (God's messenger). Her husband, children, and grandchildren adore her. She is God's classy and beloved daughter. She is truly a messenger of God who carries blessings, guidance, and important tidings. She has a quiet nature. She fits perfectly in His crown.

Introducing Jewel #7

Jewel Reschelle Means

Being a woman is her superpower. She walks in complete authority. She crushes the enemy with a warrior's mentality and strength to overcome.

The great Ms. Reschelle Means has been a real estate agent for eighteen years. She is also the co-owner of Belle Reality and Associates, which is a family-owned and operated business named after their beautiful and lovely mother. Their office is located in Spartanburg, SC. Reschelle is an amazing author. *Intruder* and *Intruder REVISED* are two of her top-selling books.

This warrior is a cancer survivor. She knocked cancer right out, with no chemotherapy or radiation treatments. Reschelle's mission was to supply herself with all natural and herbal cures along with the powerful Word of God. This God-fearing woman won with honor and victory. The books that she wrote give you the real truth and experiences she went through. Reschelle is the visionary, creator, and owner of Warriors Mentality. You can follow her on Facebook (A Warrior's Mentality), and this page is full of fire and filled with the Holy Spirit.

Reschelle cherishes and adores all children. She is incorporated at the Children's Hope Center. She brings so much value to the lives of those children, such as everyday life skills, hopes, and dreams. She is an inspirational voice for all the children. She has volunteered her time in the Big Sister, Big Brother program, and she loves her little sisters and makes time for them effortlessly. She has been a part of this program for many, many years. The love she has for her nieces and nephews is beyond infinity. The family bond she has with her mom and siblings and especially her sister is unbreakable. God uniquely designed and beautifully made Reschelle. She has a spiritual fire like no other. God admires, loves, and cherishes Reschelle. The name Reshelle signifies a gentle and nurturing nature. She fits perfectly in His crown.

INTRODUCING JEWEL #8

JEWEL LISA MOORE

She has a flare about her that no one can explain, and a uniqueness that's truly her own. The Lord has blessed her with a double portion of His anointing. The exceptional and extraordinary Jewel Lisa Moore received a bachelor's degree from Strayer University in 2009. She studied Business Administration, and she has gone on to do many things as a business entrepreneur. She is a master in all of her many skills. Lisa is owner of Land of Hope LLC, which is a real estate company for investment opportunities. Lisa is owner and operator of Moore Sweets, and she has been a bakery pastry chef for many years. She is invested in many diverse kinds of delicious desserts. She is owner of Moore Glorious Designs and Alterations, where she is a seamstress. She puts together different patterns from scratch. She is also owner of Comfort Suites, which is a business that caters to party designing for such things as birthday parties, anniversaries, private setups, and dinner for two. She decorates many different party themes. She is a crafty person in all things, very creative in any setting.

Lisa loves God with all of heart. She is the apple of His eye. Lisa has many spiritual gifts. She is a prophetess of the Lord, and she has always been a leader for Christ. She dances before the Lord in a prophetic wind. These anointed dances before the Lord our Savior are powerful, anointed, and life changing. Lisa is an intercessory prayer leader. She will always be a prayer warrior. She is the humblest ball of fire you will ever know. Lisa was a praise and worship leader, with a prophetic and anointed beautiful voice given by the Lord. The relationship she has with her son, Jonathan, is unforgettable—it is a very close bond, and blessed beyond measure. God has blessed her with an amazing, well-grounded, and blessed one and only son. She treats everyone with kindness and love. She truly loves her family. Her unique style and ways are outstanding. She stays at the feet of Jesus, operating in the prophetic realm. She is a true example of a blessing from the Lord. The name Lisa has multiple meanings: God is my oath, consecrated to God, and God's promise. Individuals with this name are often described as being intelligent, creative, and independent. What an honor! Lisa fits perfectly in His crown.

Introducing Jewel #9

Jewel Mary Keels

The best way to predict your future is to create it. "One is not born a woman, one becomes one." Let go of who you're supposed to be and embrace who you are, just like Mary Keels. She is just as lovely as she wants to be. The most wonderful and brave true-hearted Jewel Mary Keels has been employed with BMW Manufacturing for twenty-six years, and she has been found loyal. Mary is the owner and creator of Mayz Creations LLC, which is an independently owned business that creates all different fragrant soaps from scratch. Mary also makes and designs wreaths from scratch. She has very crafty hands, creating the most beautiful gift boxes, wreaths, and all sorts of handmade creations. Her work is amazing. She is also a licensed legal binding notary, and she is currently attending SCC to receive her accounting certification. This puts her in the position to book-keep and organize documents such as profit and loss statements, balancing sheets, audit books, and reports for tax purposes. She also will be qualified to make critical financial decisions by collecting, tracking, and correcting finances.

Mary is a faithful servant of the Lord. She has an extraordinary gift in singing. Her voice moves mountains. She loves praise and worship. It's deep in her soul. Mary has been married for twenty-four years to Will, and she has two smart and intelligent sons, a daughter-in-law, and two grandchildren. She is such a loving grandmother. Mary loves her family dearly. God has blessed Mary with amazing gifts. He showers her with His everlasting love. She has been found to be loyal on so many levels. The name Mary has multiple meanings, including beloved, drop of the sea, and wished for a child. The word bitterness is a reference to the sword of sorrow in Luke 2:35. This points to the cross, where Jesus died to save humanity. Mary has the biggest caring heart. She is a perfect fit in His crown.

Conclusion

Being Jewels in His crown comes with a price. It's not as easy as me just talking about a shiny diamond or being all glamorous all the time. These are some of the results you get from your obedience. You are a precious stone and jewel of great value, wealth, beauty, and durability. Malachi 3:17 states that we are His treasured possession. So the Lord has a people who are a treasured possession to Him. God is a rewarder to those who diligently seek Him. Read Hebrews 11:6. To be chosen by God in this way means you will have to be quick to obey. You will have to sacrifice some things. You are not called to go to some of the places you used to go or be with some of the people you used to be with. Everything changes because you are better. You see clearly and you practice a spirit of excellence. You love God with all your heart. Your relationship with your Father means more to you than anything else. Old habits have to go by renewing your mind. You may have to get up early to pray. You may have to turn down some meals to fast. This obedience and sacrifice brings you in direct communication with God. You do what's necessary to build a relationship with God.

Study your Bible and confess the scriptures. Live for God and die to your fleshly desires. Learn how to start again. Learn how to never quit and to stand your ground. You will have to fight in the Spirit. This is a spiritual world more than the natural. Turn on your spiritual eyes and ears and fight. "Put on the whole armor of God" (Ephesians 6:11). Speaking of humanity relates to compassion and generous behavior. "They will sparkle in his land like jewels in a crown" (Zechariah 9:16). Jewels in a crown describes how God's people will shine forth like Jewels in His land. God will deliver you and shape you into righteousness. This is called being a Jewel in His crown. This will take deliverance from God who can make all things possible. Do you believe and trust in Him? Crowns are a token of reward for believers who obey Christ. Crowns symbolize greatness and achievements. It is a sure way to have a strong connection with the Father. We are really grateful to be a chosen Jewel in His crown. The gift is for any woman that has given her life to Christ. She is ready to go to a higher level in

Him. If that is your feelings as of now, let's take it to the Father in prayer.

Heavenly Father, I bow before you and honor your holy name. I confess that I am your beloved daughter. My heart is with you, Lord. I'm asking for more of you. It is my desire to go higher in you and to have a quality relationship with you. I ask that you anoint me with your grace, mercy, wisdom, and protection. I give my life to you and ask that you direct my path and order my steps daily. Please forgive me for sins known and unknown. Let my heart, mind, and spirit harken to your Word. Transform me and create in me a clean and pure heart. Give me the heart to connect to my sister in Christ that you will bring into my life. Let me love her and cherish her always. Teach me how to be selfless and build up your cherished beloved daughter. In Jesus' name.

Encouragement

J4G encourages women to pull together. We learn and grow from one another, so invite diversity into your world. In heaven, it's already this way. Let's practice and do on earth as it is in heaven. "Your kingdom come, your will be done, on earth as it is in heaven" (Matthew 6:10). We are sisters in Christ, and we should love this. We should create a sisterhood that can't be broken. God designed us to be a blessing. Anything else isn't of God, and we should fix it immediately. Don't give the enemy a playground in your mind. Cast those thoughts down and love your sister. Celebrate her in her winning season. There is no need to be selfish and greedy. God has enough blessings to spread around. He will never run out of blessings. Know what season you are in and praise God that you will never get stuck in a season longer than His will for you. Even when God allows a winter season in your life, it's because He builds character that way. Personally, it's what I had to go through to become this woman today. There was a rainbow, and even though it rained a lot, the rainbow came eventually. I had to endure a lot, but God knew it was what I needed. That's why He allowed it. We all know pressure creates diamonds.

Speaking from a Jewel perspective, we didn't become a Jewel overnight. We all have a past where we went through a winter storm. Fitting perfectly in His crown means enduring the pressure of life's circumstances. It changed us and molded us into who we are today. Without the storms, we wouldn't grow. Think of some of the circumstances where things don't feel good at all. Children get growing pains, and it definitely doesn't feel good. Giving birth to a baby is the worst physical pain a woman will have. The end of a relationship, whether it's death or a divorce, hurts mentally and emotionally. But these are all things that cause us to grow in life. That's why women should be able to call one another for advice. We should be able to call one another for prayer. We should be able to support one another during difficult times. Seasons come and go. Through the ups and downs, we should be involved with our sisters. That's pure love and nothing more.

Open your spiritual eyes and see who God has for you. He has left no one alone. There is someone who God handpicked just for you. Don't be embarrassed to get some support during your time. If you live long enough, everyone has a time; it's just how it is. In time, you won't have the same issues as before. God will make it a distant memory, as if it never happened. It is called healing and deliverance. If you are feeling secluded, ask yourself why. Check yourself before you go pointing fingers. Ask God for a good circle of friends that love Him. He knows who His daughters are. You don't need the perfect fit, just the right fit. Your foundation starts with God to have a healthy relationship. That's the only thing that sticks.

Celebrate the gift He has given us. Explore the gift of life. It's so good to see what all He has given us. Pray for your spiritual eyes to open. You can see more than the natural eye could. Having a discerning spirit is the gift that God gives to His children. Be thankful for this gift. Take the scales off by asking God to remove them. You will have spiritual wisdom and knowledge. This will take you far in this natural world. Pray for these things daily. Surround yourself with believers. God is always on the throne. Dark will never outshine light. When you believe this, you can easily walk on water. Think about Matthew 14:17-21, when Jesus took the five loaves and two fish and fed five thousand people. God will never lose His power to do miracles. You only need to believe. Trust His perfect timing and His will. As a parent, we know more than our children. We are over them as guardians. Our Father is the same way with His children. "If you, then, though you are evil, know how to give good gifts to your children, how much more will your Father in Heaven give good gifts to those who ask him" (Matthew 7:9-11).

Resetting the Jewel in your crown.

To reset something means to set it again. You start over. Just because things didn't go as planned doesn't mean you give up. Is it easy to be a Jewel in His crown? Will you have some challenges? All relationships require maintenance and time. First you need to acknowledge that you have to be selfless to be in a relationship. You have to be fair and open-minded, knowing that sometimes you're not going to agree. It's okay to disagree and agree to disagree. We have to be respectful and caring of everyone's feelings, not taking offense to things or taking it personally.

Getting mad harbors anger and bitterness. It's the root of unforgiveness. Getting upset is understandable. It shows that you have feelings. You are human and you will experience these emotions. It's what you do with those feelings and emotions that's dangerous. When someone betrays us, we think we have the right to do something back to them. It is God's job to handle people that mishandled you. Stay in your own lane. Let God take care of this. Trust me, He can make things right. Keep your mind and heart clean. Two wrongs don't make a right. This is always the case.

Forgiveness

Being in a relationship means you are going to have to forgive. We are going to offend each other and rub each other the wrong way simply because we have a difference in opinions. We think differently sometimes. It could cause you to feel uncomfortable. Don't allow the enemy to come in and play mind games with you. He will tell you lies. Learn to not believe the lies. He loves division and knows the ways to try and destroy your relationship. This goes for any relationship, but especially for sisters in Christ. We are so powerful together. The enemy just needs an open door to come in. Don't allow this at any point and time. Know who you are and whose daughters you are. God only connects you with the best.

What are some open doors that the devil can use to get in? Examples of open doors are unforgiveness, jealousy, infidelity—basically any sin. Sin opens the door for the enemy to come in. It gives him access to come in and try to kill, steal, and destroy. Don't be fooled by him. It's so easy to be misled. Know what voice is speaking to you. You can be in love with God and still be tricked. You can be filled with the Holy Ghost and still be fooled. Be humble and pray that you are not deceived. It's a part of being imperfect.

I personally have been tricked by the enemy. I was betrayed by a close loved one. It hurt me to my core. I became unforgiven and mean, and I felt like I had the right to because they hurt me. Yes, the person was wrong for hurting me. What I did with the hurt is open the door for the enemy to bring disaster upon me. I didn't get on my knees and ask to be healed. I didn't ask for help to forgive. I disowned the person and took major offense to them. I made a lot of bad decisions out of hurt.

When we choose wrong, we have to learn from it. At some point we have to grow from our mistakes. Learn to forgive and stop holding grudges against others. Pray and ask God to help you. The spirit of offense is real. If the shoe fits, wear it. A spirit of offense means that someone might readily take offense to seemingly minor things, misinterpret intentions, and struggle to forgive others. This can lead to a negative force that can hinder relationships and spiritual growth if not addressed. Most relationships do not work if this force is present.

Lord, please remove all negative thoughts and feelings that are not from you. May your children hear your voice and know the difference. They are not tricked or deceived. Let them have a forgiving heart that holds no grudges. I pray that they shut the door and keep it tightly closed. Heal their hearts and past relationships. Teach them how to forgive easily. I pray that we repent of our sins right now in the name of Jesus. Father, please shut the voice that isn't from you. Silence the devil. I ask for the precious blood of Jesus to remove all ungodliness. We confess that today is a new day. Old things have passed away. We have become brand new. In Jesus' name. Amen.

God crowns you with glory.

Your obedience is better than your sacrifice. Sacrifice means to give up something that is valuable in order to help another person. An example is a mother who stops her teaching career to stay at home with her new baby. To sacrifice is to give freely. Another example is to pay for your children's education. Maybe you drive the same car for ten years with no car payments just to give your family the extra money needed to succeed with their plans. In Romans 12:1, Paul says to present your bodies to God as a living sacrifice. This can be done as an act of worship to God. Surrender to God and give Him your body and mind.

Sacrifice makes us who we are. If we don't capture this, we miss out on who we really are and are called to be. It is doing what is righteous, which brings spiritual conduct that honors God. Sacrifice helps us prepare to live in the presence of God. Sacrifice brings eternal rewards. It is clear that we have treasures stored in heaven. "But store up for yourselves treasures in heaven, where moths and vermin do not destroy, and where thieves do not break in and steal. For where your treasure is, there your heart will be also"

(Matthew 6:19-21). It's about having the right heart simply because it is right.

Another example of sacrifice would be a person that served in the military who has died in service to their country. A community sacrifice would be played out by helping a stranger. Personal sacrifice could also be giving up time with your friends to spend time with your family, or trusting God and turning down that promotion that requires unethical behavior. The greatest sacrifice of all time is the Father sending His Son to die for us on the cross. Sin will kill you. It's up to you to kill it before it kills you. God has the power to save you from your sins. Apply the blood of Jesus in every area of your life, especially on your doorposts: your children, marriage, parents, property, vehicles, money—nothing is off limits.

Obedience is demonstrating behaviors that are respectful and mindful of rules and laws. All people need to demonstrate obedience. The most basic and simple meaning of this word is hearing the Word of God and acting. We need to align our will to God's will, totally surrendering to Him and His authority. From a natural way of looking at it, obedience is out of duty. If you are a soldier, you obey an order from your commander and chief. Or when taking orders from your supervisor, you can be obedient out of fear of punishment.

When you follow the orders of an authority figure, it can be constructive or destructive. That's when you pray, because destructiveness is bad for society. This isn't God's will for you. Anything that harms you and puts you in danger isn't His will for you. God came that we may have abundant light. Read your Bible, trust the Holy Spirit, say yes to God, and obey God over others. Being in obedience shows that you listen deeply to God. It shows the love and respect that you have for God. Jesus was very obedient to God's plan and will. John 12:49 says, "For I did not speak on my own, but the Father who sent me commanded me to say all that I have spoken."

Some people struggle to obey God because they have a lot of sin. We all have sin, but the mission is to get deliverance. There are some who practice sin and love it, and are stuck in it. Some may not know how to get out but want out. Some are getting delivered and set free and want to obey God. Find out which best suits you and come up with an immediate plan customized for your needs with God. Everyone's plan will be different, but you need to start somewhere. The time is now, because no one is promised tomorrow.

Know what today is and live in it. Another reason for you not following God's plan and will is pride. Pride is an ugly word, in my opinion. Pride is a sin that comes from the heart and manifests in lies, violence, and self-exaltation. It is the opposite of humility and fear of God, and it leads to destruction. "Pride goes before destruction, a haughty spirt before a fall" (Proverbs 16:18). God hates the sin of pride, and destruction is brought upon those who indulge in it. Believe the Bible is true, or you will reap a harvest of disobedience and non-belief. Your life is too precious to allow those kinds of fruits in your life. Get pride out of your heart and follow Jesus' path.

Your obedience and sacrifices are sure ways to get God's crown of glory. This means that He gives ever-lasting eternal blessings for you. This is for those who are called by God and who have obeyed their calling, and have faithfully served God. This isn't as easy as said, but know that you can do all things through Christ who strengthens you (Philippians 4:13). Not by your might but His. God will give you an unfading crown of glory for your faithfulness. The crown symbolizes victory, honor, and eternal rewards for believers. It also represents the authority of Christ, the Kingdom of God, and the eternal inheritance that awaits those who love God. Seek God early, praise Him, and meditate on His Word. I want your life to change forever.

Just like you have rewards on earth, so you will get rewards in heaven. On earth, people get rewards for playing sports, making honor roll, getting perfect attendance, etc. There are also awards for movie stars, musicians, professional athletes, and more. All of these receive awards for their excellent performance, which they have trained for since they were small kids. They get knowledge and skill on what they are training in. The same thing happens in the Kingdom of God. We love Him so much that we study the Word so we can become evangelists, prophets, pastors, and praise and worship leaders. We build the Kingdom of God here on earth to help build disciples for the body of Christ. We are in preparation to become a saint. Everything you do is being recorded. He knows the heart and if you are doing this for the right reasons. You have stored treasure in heaven. If you're going to be jealous of your sister's rewards, you can't get there. Your practice is now, so clap when she wins. Get genuinely happy for church members when they get that new family car. God is watching right now of what's in your heart. Pray and ask God to take the jealousy from your heart that's been with you since a child. Anything not like love is a sin. This is the greatest command, to love your neighbor as yourself. There is so much power in obedience. Respect God and love people.

The day you were born, you made history. Everyone has a death date. It's up to you if you go to the full potential of your death date. God always has a plan (Jeremiah 29:11). The enemy has a plan to get you to sin and shorten your days on this earth. The enemy knows the Bible well. Proverbs 10:27 says, "The fear of the Lord adds length to life, but the years of the wicked are short." When you don't repent and change from your wicked ways, your choices will shorten your days on earth. You want to live a healthy life for yourself. You can't help your loved ones if you can't help yourself. Be a generational blessing and renounce family curses that's passed on through the bloodline. Stand up and be a leader. God has a calling on your life. When you answer the calling, your life looks different. The fruit you produce will show. The kind of tree you are growing is required to be watered daily. This requires the Word of God. It also consists of your faith and your faithfulness. Yield to Him and let Him direct your path. Stay in His will and pray for strength to endure. God gives us plenty of warnings. He gives us time to confess and repent. It's called mercy and grace. We don't deserve it, but He gives us unmerited favor anyway. This is our Father, and we are to love and cherish Him all the days of our life.

The Prayer of Jabez!

The prayer of Jabez is a powerful and transformational prayer in the Bible. Jabez's name means pain. This didn't stop him at all. He rose above it all despite what his name means.

"Jabez cried out to the God of Israel, 'Oh, that you would bless me and enlarge my territory! Let your hand be with me, and keep me from harm so that I will be free from pain.' And God granted his request" (1 Chronicles 4:10).

The examples in the Bible that you read about can still be true today. Do you have a faith big enough to believe in God? Jabez's prayer stands out for its heart-felt plea to God for blessing and guidance. Know who God is and that He never breaks a promise. Blessings will become curses if God's hand isn't in your life. There is only one true God. When Jabez prayed, he spoke against the testimony of his name and let go of the shame it covered him in. His prayer for God's blessing, enlargement of his territory, divine presence, and protection from evil was answered by God.

How to Make the Prayer of Jabez Our Own

Call Upon the God of Israel

Oh God, you are the Holy One of Israel. You are powerful and mighty and have called us to be set apart—holy for You. Your Holiness leads us in knowledge, justice, mercy, goodness, and love. Lord, your commands reveal your character, and we praise you today and ask that you cleanse us and remake us into the image of your Son through the power of your Spirit.

Enlarge My Territory

God, would you begin enlarging my territory today in all areas of life to claim it for your glory? Expand my borders and use my life to bring you honor and fame. Enlarge my influence in my workplace, my community, my home. May I bring you praise for all that you have done. Give me a deeper love for the lost and the broken of this world and grant me access to be used mightily for you.

Your Hand Be With Me

Thank you for setting us free and being bigger than anything we face in this life. We lay our burdens before you, every single one, for we know they're much safer in your hands than our own. God, may your hand guide me as I walk with you each step of the way. Help me to trust in your righteous right hand that strengthens and upholds me. Father God, lead me into the territory that you would have me claim for your righteousness.

Keep Me From Evil

Father God, we praise you for your love and faithfulness toward your children. We praise you for being a perfect, holy, and trustworthy God, transcending all the evil we experience here on earth. We ask that you give us eyes to see when evil is before us, hearts to hate evil, and the desire to flee from its presence. We ask that you not lead us into temptation but deliver us from evil and draw us closer to yourself. We ask for the long-expected Jesus to come quickly and make all things new. We ask these things in the precious name of Jesus. Amen.

Father God, I pray that I did exactly what you wanted me to. My ears and heart are open to hear clearly from you. Thank you for allowing me to freely write and record my thoughts and feelings. You mean more than the world to me. You have never left me or forsaken me. You always come through for me. I thank you for being all things in my life. Your unconditional love and favor runs me over. I ask that you enlarge my territory. Keep your hand with me. Keep all evil from me and my family. I love you, my Lord and Savior Jesus Christ!

ABOUT THE AUTHOR

Lashone Strickland is a lover of Jesus Christ. She is a loving wife, mother, and grandmother. She is extremely blessed for the love that her sister Jewels have shown by entrusting her to tell their story. It is a gift to write and give back to others. To learn more about her books, visit lashonestrickland.com.

JEWELS FOR GRACE

Jewels for Grace is a non-profit organization that demonstrates standards of excellence in our community.

We assist individuals in achieving their highest potential in life as they develop and grow. We support and build relationships with women as we inspire them, helping create a healthy path of life. We are a sacred gathering of women connecting, sharing, and celebrating life together, while having a compassionate heart for all people, especially other women.

To learn more about Jewels for Grace, visit our website jewelsforgrace.com.

Instagram - Jewels for Grace

Facebook - Jewels for Grace